# I Remember Nonna

# I Remember Nonna

*August R. Carnevali*

iUniverse, Inc.
New York Lincoln Shanghai

# I Remember Nonna

iUniverse books may be ordered through booksellers or by contacting:

iUniverse
2021 Pine Lake Road, Suite 100
Lincoln, NE 68512
www.iuniverse.com
1-800-Authors (1-800-288-4677)

Because of the dynamic nature of the Internet, any Web addresses or links contained in this book may have changed since publication and may no longer be valid.

The views expressed in this work are solely those of the author and do not necessarily reflect the views of the publisher, and the publisher hereby disclaims any responsibility for them.

ISBN: 978-0-595-45030-5 (pbk)
ISBN: 978-0-595-89343-0 (ebk)

Printed in the United States of America

# Contents

# *Author's Note And Acknowledgement*

I wish to dedicate this book to the memory of Ersilia Scatena, my grandmother, better known as Nonna to all 34 of her grandchildren. She was indeed a remarkable woman and it was only after she passed on in 1970 that I began to realize just how extraordinary she was. As I gave her more thought, it was later that I became aware of how much my experiences at Old Boston had so much influence on my life.

Her first husband (my grandfather) died at the age of 32 in 1914 and her second husband in 1941 leaving her to care for seven children at a time not too long after the Depression of the early 30's. When my sister Lorraine and I stayed with her at the time, I'm sure it added to her burden. But the real meaning of life, hard as it was at that time, became apparent to me years later, when I began to appreciate the real significance of what I had learned. It was Nonna who "taught me that life owed me nothing, would give me nothing if I didn't ask and gave me only what I expected of it if I did. It was that great American Poet, Jesse B. Rittenhouse who said it very fittingly in her poem, *"My Wage"*.

From the very first day at Old Boston, where Nonna lived, it was a learning experience for me because everything I encountered there was new or different. Almost every facet of my life there was affected or compromised for the better. Only three years of my life were spent with Nonna. It wasn't much time, but they were at a time when I was not only most curious about my family roots but also when I lacked answers to questions that kept popping up in my mind. For instance, who were all these relatives (and there were many) we would visit on

Sunday and holidays? My father said they were aunts, uncles and cousins. Only a few years ago I found out the extent to how many he meant when I purchased a Family Tree Program and spent four months contacting everyone and putting the charts together. The Tree went eight generations deep and had over 450 names listed.

I had intentions of putting a family tree together for some time. When I finished, I was surprised how many took an interest in what I did and before long I was receiving mail and phone calls from my cousins and other relatives around the country asking for a copy. I was glad they expressed an interest because I felt that after my first cousin generation (those who knew Nonna) was gone, much of what was remembered of Old Boston and Nonna would be gone forever. Today, only Ada and Olga of Nonna's ten children survive. It is my hope that what little I remember of Old Boston is kept alive in this book and perhaps passed on to each of my cousin's succeeding generations.

# Introduction

Old Boston! Old Boston! Where did the name come from and why? Try as I may, I couldn't find any information to research the origin of this name for that tiny hamlet located midway between Scranton and Wilkes-Barre, Pennsylvania. Of course I grew up knowing it only as "Old Boston" but it was years later when I learned of that other one (Yep! the one in Mass.) when I began to question this one. I made studies and inquiries about its origin but even the Internet failed to give me any clues. I'm inclined to believe there's a connection with those early settlers who came to that area years ago from the regions of Connecticut and Massachusetts and settled there. However, it was there, in Old Boston, where I found who I really was and that's where my behavior and values were born and honed.

I wondered why I keep reflecting back to that time with nostalgia, when it was a very unsettling period in my life. I thought about writing about Nonna and my experience in Old Boston in one continuous story but I don't remember the order in which these events happened. There were many of them. Fortunately, they happened in my pre-teen years and consequently, they were the ones that I can easily recall, that had the most effect on me as I grew up. I decided, instead, to write a series of short stories about those unforgettable episodes, as I remember them, and their influence on me. Today, it pains me to realize it's that Italian way of life I remember and love so much that I fear will soon be diluted by subsequent generations and will eventually disappear.

I was born in the town of Archbald, Pennsylvania, about eight miles northeast of Scranton, and grew up and lived there until the age of 10. Both my parents were Italian immigrants. Though my mother spoke fluent English, my father spoke broken English, so basically, I grew up in an English-speaking environment and knew little, if any, Italian. The only Italian I heard was when my parents spoke it to each other or to the relatives and that was usually only on Sundays when we paid our visits to them in our Model A Ford. But it was Old Boston that stoked my curiosity, not only because *everyone* spoke Italian to one another, but also because the way of life was so different and seemed charmingly like a back-wood environment. Though my parents were Italian and everything they did had that Italian flavor, it was there in Old Boston where it marinated for me, so to speak.

I came to liken Old Boston to Lil Abner's "Dogpatch". My maternal grandparents lived there and had ten children (Can you believe it?? I have 32 first cousins). My real grandfather died in 1914 and my grandmother remarried in 1915. My step grandfather died in 1941. I would like to point out the names of my grandmother's (Nonna in Italian) children, my aunts and uncles, because it was here where I really got to know them and thought some of their names odd at first. The first three children were those of my real grandfather. They were Theodore, Antoinette and Vienna (my mother). The rest were those of my step grandfather. They were Armand, Peter, Nello, Olga, Gildo, Elmo, and Ada. Ada is one month older than I and for a while it was a tossup as to which of us would be born first. She won by one month. My grandmother was 43 and my mother was 18 when we were born. There are some wild names there. But it was my mother's name that struck my curiosity. How did she get her name, Vienna? From what I found, it seems my grandfather, Louis Corsaletti, was in the Italian army at the time and stationed in Vienna, Austria. He loved the city so much he named my mother after its capital, or so the story goes. I point out my uncles and aunts because their presence also had a marked influence on me.

Well, the older children began getting married and when my step grandfather died in 1941, Uncle Ted (the first born) became the patriarch of the family by default. Several marriages then followed but I still wondered how the remainder of the family, was able to stay intact without a father to preside over, especially under such frugal conditions. But the real strength and cohesive force that ruled and kept the remaining family together after 1941, was Nonna. She was an amazing woman, to say the least, and she was the influence that caused (or should I say "forced"?) me to change my attitude and habits in almost all I did.

It was in 1941, not too long after my step grandfather's death, when my parents decided to find work in Waterbury, Connecticut. My father was a coal miner and hated his job and though it kept him working during the Depression, he was determined to find something different after a near-fatal mine accident. It was decided that my sister (Lorraine) and I would stay with my grandmother until they found work and an apartment in Connecticut. However, we were not told and no one said how long this would take and almost three years later I was still counting. The first day, when our parents had left, I felt that Lorraine and I were abandoned and left in a foreign land. Lorraine was only seven years old at the time so she felt very little of the fear and pain that I felt at 10 years old. But little did I realize that it would be this exposure with Nonna that would change my life completely and forever!

This was when my learning period began and it wasn't too long before I began to find out many things I never knew and answers to questions I always had. For instance there was "tripe", that delicious Italian dish that I still love with a passion. (Only much later did I find out it's made from the cow's stomach.) Then there was the bitter taste of dandelion and also the important lesson of eating bread with every meal (except pasta). Scarcely a day went by that I didn't learn or experience a new or different happening with Nonna. For example, I had a rudimentary idea that sausage casings were made from intestines, but at age 10 I didn't know what intestines were. Later, I found out from where they came but I also saw what happened to the pig. More about that will be said later. However, that didn't dampen my taste for sausage as much as the delicious meal I had one evening at my grand Aunt's (don't remember her name) when I found out afterward I ate calf's brains. Calf brains! Can you imagine? I was told I ate calf brains and didn't know it! I still can't believe it. I haven't touched it since. That's the problem with Italian food. It's so deliciously camouflaged, it's impossible, at times, to tell by taste alone, what one is eating!

So, I never knew when surprises would pop up at Nonna's, especially at the dinner table. But I was quickly becoming acclimated and after awhile, my experiences there became more routine and less suspicious.

To write about *all* my experiences and lessons I learned from Nonna would require many more pages than I present with this book. But I write these that had a profound influence on me. Saying that, I now invite you on a visit to Nonna's farm in Old Boston, a nostalgic part of my life.

# Old Boston 101

I could see that anything that happened at Nonna's was going to make an impression on my life since everything was a new experience. The first night in Old Boston made the first big impression on my life when I found that I would be sharing a bed with my uncle Elmo. I had never slept with anyone before and I felt very squeamish about it. As it turned out, I spent almost the whole first night trying to avoid being hit by his massive legs every time he moved. I had a major problem here. However, after the second night of the same sparring, I decided something had to be done and quickly. Just before retiring that third evening, as I stood staring at the bed giving it more thought, the solution hit me like a flash. Eureka! *I had it!* Instead of sleeping *under* the bed sheet, I would sleep *on top* of it between it and the outside blanket. Elmo would be *under* it and the blanket. At first I was reluctant to try it because I didn't think that such an arrangement would go unnoticed. I felt there must be a flaw there somewhere. But the question in my mind was if Elmo would accept that arrangement. I decided not to tell him and let him find out for himself. I would plead ignorance if he did. I put it to the test and I don't know if he ever found out because he never said anything. So I let it be. To this day, no one ever knew I slept on *top* of the sheet and Elmo *under* it. As a result, the twain was never able to meet and sleeping with Elmo was never a problem again.

Lorraine shared the next bedroom with Ada and every morning came the wake-up call at seven o'clock from Nonna downstairs, *"Ada, Lorena (Lorraine), E tempo di alzarsi! (Its time to get up!)"*. At this time, several minor chores that needed tending were done before school or breakfast. While Lorraine took these "before breakfast" chores in stride, I took issue with them before my "hard bread" breakfast. However, the rule of Nonna's law prevailed and a number of times my breakfast had to wait. From this I learned later in life when I worked that sometime certain matters needed attention first and must be given priority. At Nonna's, it happened more often than not.

I must mention at this point that my biggest problem at first was trying to understand Nonna when she spoke Italian. I didn't understand a single word in Italian and it was very frustrating when she talked to me. Ada was my translator every time she spoke to me. I had to keep asking her, "What did she say?" But after three years at Old Boston, I had come a long way. I became "Italianized."

Understanding Italian was one problem I overcame. Understanding Nonna was different. After breakfast of the second day I was standing near the outdoor stone oven Nonna used for baking bread, when she came out of the kitchen upstairs at the house and stood on the porch and started yelling *"Agoo, oh Agoo!"* Again she called *"Oh Agoo"*. For the life of me, I didn't know what she was doing. To me it seemed like she was trying to imitate the klaxon horn on a model A Ford. Strange woman, I thought! She turned her head and saw me looking at her and gave me a tongue lashing yelling *"Perche' non mi risponde?"* (Why don't you answer me?). I was confused! My name is Augie and everyone calls me Augie. No one ever told me my name was changed to Agoo. I didn't like the name but I wasn't going to debate the point with Nonna, so I responded to the name "Agoo", when she called me.

My sister Lorraine seemed to accept the transition much better than I but then again, she was only seven years old. At first, I felt totally abandoned and it was hard for me to accept the many issues I knew would come. And they weren't long in coming. The first morning I sat down for breakfast at Nonna's; I suspected it would be the harbinger for things to come, and it was. Her recipe for making morning coffee was a model of brevity. She boiled water in a saucepan and when it came to a boil she added several spoons of coffee and let it simmer to the strength desired. That's it! Then the coffee was poured through a tea strainer (Yep, a tea strainer!) into our waiting cups Next came the sugar and the canned evaporated milk (Borden's I believe). I looked at the coffee and it was plain to see that the tea strainer was not the way to go. It only blocked the coffee grounds that were larger than the holes in the strainer. When the remaining smaller grains floated lazily to the surface of the coffee or sank, it was obvious to see that the coffee clearly needed help. So, the first few minutes at breakfast each morning were devoted to removing the grains that floated. It would be hard to label this coffee "Good to the last drop" because not all the grains floated. The rest sank and were piled on the bottom of the cup. One was always careful when he drank a cup of coffee at Nonna's. We *never* drank to the last drop. And as I stared at the coffee in my cup for the first time, it was hard for me to believe that this might to be our rock bottom expectation for breakfast and felt it had to get better than this. But I was dead wrong. It didn't get better. This was *it!* When Nonna handed me a slice of hard bread from the evening meal the night before, this had to be the "0" on the 0 to 10 scale of "tasty breakfasts". This was surely not a portent of better times to come and I became careful in my expectations after that. So that was our breakfast; a hard crust of bread dipped into a strong cup of coffee. Breakfast was the same fare every day. Food was not wasted at Nonna's.

# *Waste Not, Want Not*

Mom, without question, made the tastiest Italian meals that were ever concocted in a kitchen. She had a way of taking the simplest of foods and even camouflaging leftovers and turn them into some of the most appetizing meals I have ever eaten. In my eyes she was a marvel in the kitchen. But unfortunately, Mom always doted on us and as a result we had poor eating habits. I never realized how poor they were until I went to live with Nonna. Of course her food was delicious, but her format or approach was different. She always added her own personal touch to the cuisine. For example, pork and beans, (I remember seeing the Campbell label. They must have been around in 1940/41) was a popular dish with everyone and Nonna not only added fried onions, which made them very tasty, but also a finely chopped red pepper. Now, eating one of Nonna's garden grown hot peppers was tantamount to flirting with fire! The very fingers burned when the peppers were picked from the plants. I remember the first mouthful of Nonna's beans that I tasted, was akin to sucking on a hot poker. And no matter how hot the beans were going in, they were *always* hotter coming out! It was clearly a fiery undertaking that was painful on both ends.

There was a number one rule in Nonna's kitchen: everything on the plate, once taken, must be eaten. Food was not wasted. Rule number two stated that bread must be eaten with everything (except pasta). An addendum to Rule number two was: the bread must go into the mouth *first*. Can you believe that? People don't believe me when I tell them! I can remember very clearly being corrected a number of times by Nonna (Cross my heart!). Now strangely enough, to this day, I eat bread with everything (except pasta) but only sometimes do I put the bread in my mouth first, (Even though I can feel Nonna watching!)

I must tell this experience Lorraine had with Nonna that she remembers to this day, because it was *so* funny when it happened. Nonna was certainly not without a sense of humor and would pull a practical joke on one of us at times, without warning, when she saw the opportunity. This one day at supper, Lorraine was just about finished with her meal when Nonna slipped a cooked hot pepper on her plate without her noticing. Now Lorraine knew full well about the first rule of eating everything so thinking it was a sweet pepper on the plate, with her fork she put the whole pepper in her mouth. Suddenly her eyes bolted wide open. She jumped from the chair, spit out the mouthful and made a beeline to the sink gagging and drinking water as fast as it could come from the faucet. Well, Nonna laughed so hard that she could hardly catch her breath. The strange result of this incident is that Lorraine, to this day, loves hot cherry peppers and eats them with no restraint. Unbelievable!

There are many first time experiences I had in Nonna's kitchen but they are too numerous to mention, so I'll touch only on those few I remember best that made an impact. The one experience I will never forget that stands out most clearly in my mind was the dandelion salad incident. When I recount the story to anyone, they find it hard to believe it happened as I describe and when I think of it, so do I. But it *did* happen! I like salad and I can't ever remember disliking any my mother used to make. But I don't ever remember her making dandelion salad so I will say that I don't remember eating it. Well, this one evening for dinner I made the mistake of taking dandelion salad at Nonna's. My first mouthful immediately told me I made a wrong choice. It tasted very bitter and I had a hard time swallowing my mouthful. I realized immediately that I would be in direct violation of Nonna's cardinal rule number one, (eat everything on the plate). What to do? What to do?

I decided not to eat the salad, which did not stand well with Nonna. In very clear terms she let me know that my decision was not an option. I was to finish my salad before I ate anything else. Of course, I thought, she couldn't be serious. After all, dandelion belonged to the weed family.

I gave it a moment of thought and concluded that she wouldn't let me starve. So I forfeited what was left of my meal for the evening. Next morning as I waited for the coffee and my piece of hard bread for breakfast, Nonna put the salad in front of me. I just couldn't believe it! Did she really expect me to eat it now for breakfast? When she gave me nothing else and I just sat there, I began to get the message. I had to eat the dandelion before I got anything else! It began to get painfully obvious that this issue was starting to get out of hand. Hard bread for breakfast began to start looking good at this point. There was no way I was going to eat those wilted, stale, weeds for breakfast! It was only later that I realized she was only expressing her authority on the matter, but at the time I thought she was *really* paddling with one oar! However, I must admit that it was then when I learned a very important lesson. The strength of any law or rule lied in the actions of those willing to enforce its rule, and Nonna certainly didn't have that problem. Nevertheless, a crisis loomed. Have you ever seen dandelion or any leafy vegetable that has marinated in wine vinegar for 16 hours? It loses all of its crisp characteristics and becomes as soft, limp and slimy as an overcooked noodle. I got up and left the table. I must have had Ada's sympathy because she didn't have that usual smile she always carried. When it was time for lunch, I couldn't help feeling this premonition of what to expect. I sat down and I was right! I was served the same fare. Well, that was it! This nonsense had gone too far! I decided I had enough of that crazy woman and I wasn't going to play any more of her stupid games. I took a deep breath and in one fell swoop I swallowed all the dandelion. While I sat there coughing and gagging and trying to catch my breath, Nonna looked at me, started laughing like crazy (a "welcome back" laugh, not a sardonic one.) and with a big grin on her face gave me my lunch. As an ironic note, I would like to add that today I love dandelion salad, (fresh) and it *is* my favorite.

I must make mention of Nonna's bread that she baked quite often. Outside, about 50 or 60 feet from the house was the stone oven where Nonna baked the bread for the family. She used a large zinc-plated tub that measured about two feet by about 12" deep. She would empty a large bag of flour into it with the necessary yeast and knead the large mass until it was ready for rising. This was enough for 10 or 15 loaves. The bread was put into bread pans and let rise again. Then she would begin by setting fire to the wood that had been stacked inside the oven. When burned through, the oven got extremely hot inside and the ashes were scooped out with a long wooden hoe. The bread, ready in their bread pans, was then put inside the hot oven to bake. It was at this point when that heavenly smell of Nonna's baked bread wafted throughout the neighborhood. One day when I was standing watching her take the bread out of the pans, she told me to go up to the kitchen and bring her a knife. She took the knife and cut about a two inch thick slice off the end of one loaf and handed it to me. Hanging just inside the door were several strings of garlic from the garden, drying out. She broke off a thick clove from one, peeled off the outer skin and handed it to me. For a moment I looked at the garlic and then at her. Yep. She wanted me to eat it. Taking a bite of the fresh warm bread and a small bite of the garlic, I tasted garlic bread, Nonna style, for the first time. It was delicious. When I eat garlic-bread in an Italian restaurant today, I can't help but think that perhaps, it had its humble beginnings that day in Nonna's oven.

# The Backhouse

There were many unforgettable incidents that happened at Old Boston that I probably will never forget and too numerous to write but some were so profound that I remember them like they happened yesterday. This was one of them. I'll assume you know what a "backhouse" or "outhouse" is. I wanted to write it phonetically as an Italian would call it but I don't know how to spell it. It's the outside toilet that I believe everyone in Old Boston had before indoor toilets became fashionable. Before I go any further, let me describe the setting for this John that existed at the time and how it gave birth to this episode.

Nonna's house was quite new. It was built on the site of her previous house that had burned down (as I understand the story.). I vaguely remember this home when it had just been built because I recollect walking through the empty rooms. I must have been near four years old at the time. The backhouse must have been built for the previous home because the new home had a bathtub and toilet. Now, Nonna made it clear that under no circumstances was the toilet in the house to be used at any time. We were to take a piece of paper (Yep. A piece of paper!), and use the backhouse located down below the house in the thicket.

I decided to take a look at this gem and what I saw would make the Munster's home look like a page out of "Better Homes and Gardens". The Backhouse was very dilapidated and grown over with weeds, inside and out, and covered with webs of every kind. This was certainly a carryover of a previous era. At first glance I could see it was the home of several species of spiders and bugs, guarded by the local bees. This definitely posed a real dilemma for me because I never roughed it. Realizing that at some time or other I would have to patronize the premises, I took a long tree branch and began sweeping and clearing the area of webs. It was later after several uses that I found out that inside and underneath the seat were more occupants expressing their hostility and forcing me, several times, to make a hasty exit to the outdoors and elsewhere on Nonna's property. When that became too bothersome, I had to chance using the toilet in the house making sure I never spent more than five or ten minutes in there. I felt if I could use the toilet fast enough, I could zip in, quickly do my thing and zip out before anyone ever knew. Of course, this was before I heard of "Murphy's Law". I felt that I wouldn't have enough time to get caught in the short time span between the two zips. But I *did*.

This experience with the toilet was great training for me in crisis management. It happened one day when my needs came very suddenly and I had to act immediately. I definitely did not want to use the Backhouse so I decided to use the toilet in the house. I quickly checked everywhere I thought Nonna would be but couldn't find her so I figured the chance of her appearing for the next few minutes was too remote to happen. Thinking it was safe, I chose to make an attempt to use the toilet in the house so I went in and locked the toilet door. So far, so good! I no sooner began to perform my needs when I heard

Nonna coming up the steps outside the kitchen door speaking to some-one. I totally panicked and thought for sure I was dead! My pulse rate went up ten points while I was making my peace with God when the screen door to the kitchen creaked open and slammed shut. Evidently, the good Lord was siding with Nonna! A few seconds later she tried opening the door to the toilet but I had the door locked, of course. A moment later she banged hard on the door yelling "*Chi sta li dentro?*" (Who is in there?). With frightened voice I replied, "It's me". Now in a loud voice she yells "*Scappa via!*" (Get out). Scappa via? Was she kid-ding? Get a load of this picture: there I was sitting on the toilet and this crazy lady was banging on the door yelling "scappa via". This was a seri-ous problem! I was to either jump out the window or face dire conse-quences. The window was too far from the ground to jump and I was in the middle of my thing. What happened next I could only attribute to a moment of panic and confusion. I had to think fast and go for broke! Suddenly, I had an idea that may be a win-win situation. In a flash I concluded what I was doing, unlocked the door, dashed out and on the run, kissed Nonna on the cheek, said: "thank you" and kept run-ning. I felt she couldn't be mad at me for kissing her and if she could, she'd have to catch me. Though I expected it to happen, Nonna never brought up the incident and I just simply behaved as though it never happened. I think the kiss caught her off guard. And like the old adage "let sleeping dogs lie", I did. However, I still chanced to use that toilet when necessary. My fear of the backhouse was greater than that of Nonna.

# A Penny Saved

As I mentioned, the house in Old Boston was a replacement of the previous one that burned down and furniture was gradually purchased for it. Aunt Olga was involved in this incident. She got married in 1942 and I don't remember if this occasion happened before or after she lived in Old Boston. But it was she who gathered me, Ada, Lorraine and Elmo together in the kitchen upstairs one day to lay the law down, for the new (or used) refrigerator that was purchased. Among several things she said, was the fact that it cost a penny every time anyone opened the refrigerator door. By this she was trying to emphasize to us not to open the door to the refrigerator needlessly. But in my mind, I really thought payment of a penny was required to open the door.

Well, it had to happen! The day came when I was in the basement kitchen with Nonna when she told me to go upstairs and get something from the refrigerator. I stood there and looked at her waiting for her to give me the penny to pay to open the refrigerator door (I didn't know who to pay the penny but I assumed it was aunt Olga). She looked at me and said, '*Cosa stai asppetando?*" (What are you waiting for?). Holding my hand out I said, "I need a penny". That remark took Nonna by surprise. Apparently she thought I was trying to shake her down. Her outburst at that point was more menacing than the lack of a penny so I hightailed it upstairs, got what she wanted and hoped Aunt Olga wouldn't find out.

Another incident involving Aunt Olga at the time happened when Uncle Joe (aunt Olga's husband) had stayed overnight at Nonna's with his sister Marilyn. For breakfast we had our usual fare of bread and coffee. But aunt Olga gave Marilyn a buttered piece of soft bread. Marilyn quickly noticed the difference in our fares and when no one was looking quietly slipped me her buttered piece of bread (I must have looked at her bread longingly). Though we seldom crossed paths again, we became fast friends. No one knew about it but that was the best breakfast I had at Nonna's that I could remember.

# The Garden

Nonna's overall property was quite large and I would guess several acres. She had a good-sized vegetable garden with a varied assortment of vegetables growing there that she would can for the year. I figured it wouldn't take too long for me to learn how to do the weeding That surprised me a little. I was told I would be doing that and other cares that the garden required, (after all, how smart does one have to be to pull weeds from the ground?). Ada, again, was my mentor and she showed me that pulling the weeds out was only part of the job. I couldn't imagine what else could possibly be done to weeds. Then Ada showed me that pulling weeds had developed into an art. The dirt had to be shaken loose from the roots of each handful of weeds and the weeds put into the wooden basket we were lugging (I wondered why we had it). Of course, another question popped into my head. Why put the weeds in the basket and not just leave them uprooted on the ground? I felt a little apprehensive about this point and sensed another lesson was about to emerge

As I said, every experience at Nonna's seemed to be a new one and the answer to the mystery of the "weeds in the basket", I knew, would not be long in coming. Weeding the garden was only the tip of the "weed iceberg". When we had finished, we carried the filled basket up to the cellar in the house and Nonna sat me down in front of this wooden block. Then she grabbed a handful of weeds and with a large machete, showed me how she wanted me to chop them. Now, why in the world would she want the weeds chopped? It seemed each stage of the weed cycle was a prelude to another step. Nonna came through with a reason as usual. The chopped weeds would be mixed with mash and water and served as food for the ducks (She had about 15 of them). I thought this was absolutely amazing! When I saw how this was done, I marveled at the self-serving efficiency of this procedure. The ducks ate when the garden was weeded for the mash. But they had to be fed every day so naturally, the garden was always weeded to keep the ducks fed. Perfect! Nonna had, at the same time, both a weed less garden and happy ducks!

Though I learned to do many different chores in the garden, there were only a few I found repulsive and took a while to tolerate. The leader of this group was the string beans. The beans grew on vines that were tied to upright poles stuck in the ground and were taller than I. It seemed there were certain bugs that had a strong attraction for bean leaves and not only chewed on them but also nested and laid tiny clusters of eggs on the underside of the leaf. Though I respected "the right to life", even for bugs, my attitude has always been "Live and let live". But Nonna's philosophy was "Not on my farm!" and she had Ada instruct me how to seek out and destroy these little varmints in their nest. It was a simple enough procedure. I would examine the underside of each leaf and if there were bugs or egg clusters there, I would fold the leaf over on itself and squish them (for lack of a better description).

Therefore, *all* the leaves had to be examined and this operation had to be performed on all of those that had these bugs or eggs. So one could see very easily that squishing could easily become a long-term project since all leaves had to be examined, and there were many plants with many leaves Now, Nonna had several rows of bean plants so when I lost whatever reservations I had about doing this, I became quite fast and an expert squisher in no time at all (I always kid Ada about how well she taught me to become an expert squisher).

Many other chores I learned to do in that basement. It was there where I learned from where the title of "Pennsylvania Coal Cracker" came. The Scranton-Wilkes-Barre area was in the heart of the anthracite coal region. The coal was mined there and was extremely hard and burned with a hot blue flame. It was easily found everywhere where it was mined or transported and one easily found pieces laying near the breakers or on the roadside where coal trucks passed. Most families in that region never bought but picked and burned coal for heating and cooking. Nonna was no exception. Uncles Elmo, Gildo and Pete may have supplied the coal but now Nonna needed a coal cracker. I was given a claw hammer and basically told to crack the coal to a certain size. It was a simple enough task but it was the large chunks that gave me problems. Anthracite coal is very hard and hitting a chunk with the hammer, most times, did nothing more than to send chips flying in all directions. Anyone from the Scranton, Wilkes-Barre region of Pennsylvania knows very well the sting of these little suckers when trying to crack that coal. After awhile, with practice though, it was possible to tell, like a diamond cutter, where to strike the blow to break it open. I could count on staying in practice cracking coal at least once a week at Nonna's. This might have been good experience for a diamond-cutter apprentice.

# The Hen House

Most everything that happened to me in Old Boston seemed disturbing at first and after awhile, I felt I had run the gauntlet of stressful episodes. But again, I was wrong because they kept popping up unexpectedly and this was one of them.

Nonna had a Hen House down the back (which we know better as a Chicken Coop) where approximately 20 chickens roosted. Unlike the ducks that were free to roam near their little pond, the chickens were less trustworthy and were penned in because they laid their eggs in nests in the coop and also were harder to control if they were free. Well, Nonna, at times, would send me down to the coop with a basket or pan to collect the eggs. But here was the difficulty. Collecting the eggs from the nests that had no chickens in them was no problem. But if I had to feel under the chicken for the eggs, they knew I was eggnapping and showed their hostility by violently pecking my hand. Lorraine had the same problem when she was told to collect them. I learned that I could distract them with one hand and grab the eggs with the other. But then there was the rooster, the only one there, who thought I was trying to muscle in on his harem and would come at me with wings raised, neck extended and threatening me with loud rooster swear words. I would scramble to the door each time, barely escaping his fury. Only through guile and deviousness after several attempts, was I able to collect all the eggs.

But that wasn't the whole story with the chicken coop. The day came when Nonna felt I was ready to advance to the next plateau in my coop training and it was the chicken droppings under the roost that figured in my schooling. These droppings released a strong pungent ammonia odor that penetrated my whole being including my clothes. Sometimes it would last for several days and scrub as I may, there was always a slight telltale odor left. I was given a typical coal shovel and shown how to scrape up the chicken droppings (which were hard on the floor at this stage) and dump them in the basket (yep, the basket. This told me to expect a new lesson). The problem here was that the roost (where the chickens spent most of their cackling, gossip, nest time) was three feet off the floor. To clean under the roost, I had to bend over and go underneath to scrape the floor. As luck would have it, those hens cared little about me under them, so I learned quickly to shoo them out of the coop into the yard before scraping. The scrapings were hard and later broken up into small pieces and distributed around the garden plants as fertilizer. This chore, of course, was the pre-requisite for the next lesson that was to follow. How we fertilized the plants with the chicken droppings I leave to your imagination, because that's a story that I *really* want to forget!

# To Market, To Market

At first I had no intention of including this chapter of the pig slaughter Nonna had in Old Boston. But it was the only one like it that happened while I was there and I include it because from it, I learned from where many of the different Italian Pork products came. Being an animal lover, I will treat this chapter lightly and vaguely where the description becomes too graphic.

Nonna had two or three pigs in a pen down the back yard. I had so little to do with them that I barely remember attending to them at all. But what I do remember is the vivid slaughter of one of the pigs. It all happened in the downstairs cellar, off the kitchen near the furnace where it took all the strength of four or five guys to eventually subdue the pig. They did this by first looping a cord around the lower jaw and over the head. I guess this was done to prevent any movement of the mouth while its blood drained. Front legs were tied together and then hoisted by the rear legs to a hook in the wall. I would guess the animal weighed around 350/400 pounds. It must have been quite an undertaking for four guys trying to manage such a feat with the pigs' frantic,

27

howling squeals and then hanging it up side down by the back feet from that hook, while it struggled. A zinc-plated bucket was placed under its head and I got goose bumps when the pig's throat was punctured. Aside from the initial shock and hysterical thrashing about of the pig, it struck me odd to see it, after a few moments, suddenly just hang there quietly while the blood drained into the pail. I suspect the pig went into shock from loss of blood and just quietly, with no movement, die.

The carcass hung there for about 45 minutes with no more blood draining, when the stomach was slit from the hip at the top down to the neck on the bottom. I will always remember what I saw next. The stomach opened like a zipper and all the internal organs spilled out into the large pan on the floor. Another thing I noticed was the steam it generated. It must have been done during the cool of winter.

After several hours of butchering and sorting of the various innards, I really only recognized the fatback with which Nonna cooked. Later came the bacon and pork chops. The intestines were removed, emptied, turned inside out and scraped clean with a sharp knife. Then they were reversed again and washed clean. They seemed to be about 20 feet long.

After eight or ten hours later of work (The guys worked from morning into late evening), I began to recognize the prosciuttos and lonsas that were made, those delicious Italian hams so common on Italian dinner tables. The hams that were prepared were seasoned, salt-cured and air-dried. The sausage meats were ground and stuffed into the casings and all made ready for curing in the wine cellar, which was kept, for about 9/10 months, at a constant 65/70 degrees for curing. But this temperature can vary.

The wine cellar was a concrete building off to the side of the house that contained three barrels of wine Nonna had made during the year. This wine was sold to the local miners and inhabitants and served as additional income for her. The only thing left, I remember, was a distinctively, strong unpleasant odor that was left behind after all was finished. I don't think it's necessary to cover much more of this story because each farm animal suffered its own peculiar demise when prepared for the dinner table. Whenever I have any of these foods for dinner though, I think back to those days with Nonna. I learned a lot at Old Boston.

# *The Nickelette*

The Nickelette was a movie shown weekly in the large empty room above the local Italian Social Club down the road. (There's no correct spelling for the word since, I believe, Nonna made it up. She called it a "Nickeletto"). For a nickel (hence, the name.), a person could watch a movie and an action chapter from a projector with sound that was brought in by an entrepreneur looking to make a few bucks. The screen was nothing more than a bed sheet hung against the wall. There were no chairs so the few grown-ups that attended stood against the wall and the children sat on the floor between the projector and the screen. The movie was shown primarily for the children and teenagers so there was always a full house. As Spartan as all this seemed, it was still the high-point for the children's activities in the area and kids would come from all around with a sandwich or snack to eat during the show. The only time there was a problem in such close quarters when the room was full was when someone in the room had let out wind. It was so intense at times that the windows were opened and fans turned on. Luckily, the culprit was never found.

The room was always filled to capacity on Saturday evenings with all the kids on the floor. It was something they looked forward to every week, and God help that projectionist if he didn't show up. One Saturday evening during the movie, the film ripped and the lights came on. There was a near riot until they spliced the film.

Now, Nonna was the only source for the admission fee and boy, did she use it to her advantage. She got many chores accomplished because she knew we made sure we did as we were told for everything and we were careful not to upset her. One time she made me clear out all the rocks in the small garden above the road. I spent the whole day busting my chops to make sure they were all taken out. I wasn't going to jeopardize my nickel Nonna was going to pay me! I still remember her reaching into the pocket of her apron and taking out her little leather change purse and handing me a nickel (Lorraine recently informed me that she has that little leather change purse!). Nonna was appeased and I got the nickel Of course, there were two times when I messed up and was punished but I had a good run on good behavior. So, it was important not to lose the admission fee.

A nickel may not seem like much now but I remember at Poppel's grocery store up the road that 5 cents bought a lot. I remember a penny bought five Tootsie rolls or three sticks of bubblegum, or two lollipops etc. So, with five cents I could get a small bag full of candy. Now, *that* was power!

# The Entrepreneur

Each of my aunts and uncles had their own peculiar ways and eventually all added their own particular flavor to my experiences at Old Boston, but it was one of Elmo's entrepreneurial schemes that involved me directly in a plan to make money for him.

Elmo had a makeshift shoeshine box he had made and would quite often go over to the Italian Social Club to make some money shining shoes. Here is where working men, sometimes in their work clothes, would pay 20 cents for a shoe shine that meant squat and did very little to improve their appearance. But yet there was a market there. I'm sure their real desire for the shine was to help Elmo make a little money. Well, Elmo came up to me one day and asked if I would be interested in making some money working for him shining shoes. I got really excited as visions of all this money rained down on me. I told him I had no shoe shine kit. Not to worry, he said. Naturally I said yes. He would lend me his kit and I only had to learn to shine shoes. He gave me a quick lesson and took me over to the club with him and, as luck would have it, he shined the shoes of one person there. He made 20 cents in about six or seven minutes. Think of the candy that could buy! I couldn't believe how simple it was.

Here was the catch. I would use his kit and keep a nickel for each pair of shoes I shined. The rest was his. I tried this every day for one week and made ten cents. There was no market, it seemed, for shiny shoes But Elmo made 30 cents and didn't have to lift a finger. It was obvious that working hard was not the way to make a killing in the shoeshine business. My visions evaporated in a flash.

Elmo was four years older than I but he always treated me as an equal and would include me in many of his activities. He would take me fishing or swimming, taught me many things and seemed to enjoy my company. I never forgot this one particular day when a discussion of "babies" came up and he asked me if I knew from where they came. I was only 10 years old and very naïve about the subject. I didn't want him to think that I thought storks delivered them. Admitting I didn't really know, he told me and I was dumbstruck. The very act that I was taught was sinful, as a Catholic, Elmo said was necessary for procreation. I wouldn't believe it and Elmo had me ask two of his cronies and they gave the same answer. Did the good Lord approve such an exception and tell His people to go forth, sin and inhabit the world? This explanation was probably the hardest thing for me to believe and it was some time before I discovered the fallacy in my argument and accepted the idea.

But as I said, Elmo and I did many things together. One day he was going to take me swimming with him to the Small Dam, which was located about four miles away in Westminster, the next town. A set of railroad tracks, no more than 900 yards far from Old Boston, passed the dam in Westminster. As we walked through the woodland, we came to the tracks that climbed slightly up a slope. Elmo stopped and listened for a moment and said that a freight train was coming and we may be able to hop onto it. I didn't know what he was talking about but I didn't like the sound of the word "hop". Soon we could see the train in the distance and it began to slow down climbing the incline. Elmo was going to hop on first and I was to do exactly as he did. When the Engine came abreast and passed us, it was still going faster than we could run but Elmo leaped and grabbed the bottom rung of the ladder on front of the freight car and pulled himself up and hung on. It was my turn now and as the train slowly outpaced me Elmo was yelling for me to jump on but the ladder rung was chest high and hard to grasp as I ran. I was terrified. I made a leap and grabbed the rung but my feet were being dragged on the rocks of the track bed. I managed to pull my feet up and hang on for dear life about three feet above the ground for the next 15 minutes. It was then that I was convinced that it wasn't bravado I lacked. Elmo was simply a nut and I was stupid for listening to him.

As we rolled along, the thought of getting off terrified me. The wheels rolling on the rails made a loud clackety clack noise, which scared me. Elmo told me to jump off when I saw him jump two cars ahead but it seemed to me we were going too fast and I began to have reservations about listening to him. But then it happened. Elmo jumped off. I steeled myself and prepared to jump but couldn't. My car approached Elmo standing looking at me and as I passed him, he went ballistic! He started running alongside yelling "Jump! Jump", but I was too afraid. I knew my problem was becoming grave as he began to fade farther and farther behind me in the distance. If I didn't jump, God knows where I would end this trip. But I was in luck! A patch of high weeds was approaching so I prepared to jump there. I did and tumbled like a ball down the side of the track bed. Elmo caught up to me and was furious but I didn't care. *I was alive! Alive!* I could have wound up in Pittsburgh or somewhere.

As I said, Elmo and I did many things together but one day he unwittingly made me a partner in crime. Nonna did a lot of vegetable and fruit canning in Old Boston. Aside from the garden, her property was riddled with apple and peach trees. Along with blueberries we picked, she had an assortment of canned fruits that was a treat when she served them. The canned goods were located on shelves in the crawl space in the next cellar. One day Elmo came to me and asked if I would do him a favor. He wanted me to go into the cellar and hand him a quart bottle of canned peaches through the cellar window. I thought nothing of it and said sure. I went in and got a quart of peaches and gave it to Elmo waiting outside the locked basement window. I unlocked it and gave it to him. He thanked me and told me to make sure I locked the window again and then he was gone, that quick. I did so and stood there wondering what happened and why he wanted the peaches and then to make sure the window was locked again. Suddenly I realized I was duped and made a partner in a crime! The only difference was that I didn't share in the plunder. I quickly high-tailed out of there before Nonna saw me and wondered why I was there. For that moment, I shuddered when I thought what would have happened to me if she caught me.

# The Con Man

As I mentioned, each of my aunts and uncles left their own peculiar impressions on me but Gildo's was perhaps, the most exceptional. Though he was a favorite Uncle of mine, I felt he was the con man of the siblings. I don't know why, but I was fooled several times by him. So that makes him an extremely gifted con man or me very stupid! The one, which I remembered best, involved the soda truck that made deliveries to the Social Club.

It happened one afternoon while I was watching a Bocce game in the back of the clubhouse. A large soda truck had pulled up and parked in the parking lot near the entrance to the building. It was the kind of truck that had cases of quart bottles of soda on the two sides of the truck, leaning back and facing outward for easy access. I was surprised when I was tapped on the shoulder and turned to see uncle Gildo. He wanted to talk to me and asked me if I would be interested in making ten cents. Wow! 10 cents! That was a bonanza for a kid who never sees money so I practically shouted, "yes, yes"! So Gildo brought me nearer to the truck and told me the driver had just gone into the clubhouse to get the order for soda and would come back out to get it from the truck. When he does, he will deliver it back inside and as soon as he's gone I'm to grab a bottle and go down to the tracks behind the clubhouse and take it up to Nonna's garden where he'll be waiting. I was so taken with the thought of making 10 cents that it didn't occur to me that I would be stealing.

The driver came out, put two cases of soda on the hand truck and delivered them inside the club just as Gildo predicted. I calmly walked over and took out a bottle of Coca Cola and very coolly walked down to the tracks below. As I approached Nonna's garden I could see Gildo waiting for me. I went up to him and gave him the bottle of soda and he handed me a wine glass he was holding. Apparently, he went to the house and got a glass before I came. With a bottle opener (now where did that come from?) he opened the bottle, and filled the glass I was holding. So I took it and waited for the 10 cents. But it wasn't forthcoming so I asked him for it. He told me a glass of soda at the club costs 10 cents and that the glass of soda he gave me was payment. for the dime he said he'd give me. I wasn't too swift at 10 years old but I knew something was wrong here. It wasn't much later that I realized I was conned. And the soda was even warm! From that day I became suspicious with anything Gildo told me.

# Conclusion

My life at Nonna's, in the beginning, was very unpleasant because it was a very radical change in my lifestyle and because I missed my parents. But after three years, my expectations became weak and salvation seemed remote. Lorraine and I gradually became molded to that way of life, which, at that point, became very routine. Then suddenly, one weekend, it happened! Like a thunderbolt it came out of the blue. Our stay with Nonna came to a swift and sudden end when Lorraine and I were told we were leaving for Connecticut that weekend with my parents. What a surprising shock that was! No one had ever said anything or even hinted we were going to leave. When we finally realized it was true and got over our disbelief, I was right! I *did* hear a heavenly choir in the background confirming the good tidings singing hallelujah.

Next day as departure time drew near, I knew life would never be the same for me because I was a different functioning person at this point, and I began to get an uncomfortable feeling about leaving. It seems that as much as I wanted to go, I was going to miss Nonna. Why? I didn't know. I imagine it's much like that empty feeling one gets with the silence after a train has roared past for several minutes. Life was very hard under her tutelage. She was a very stern woman but it was later that I realized that it was her tough and hard-hitting approach to daily life that was necessary to keep the family together. Today, I marvel how she was able to daily feed such a large family or how she was able to meet her living expenses. When we got to Connecticut and renewed our life there, I never forgot her and looked forward to visiting her. Years later, when we didn't visit as often, I would make certain to send greeting cards for holidays or occasions that arose. I was very glad to find out later how much she looked forward to receiving them. When I did have the opportunity to visit her, I was surprised that she was so happy to see me. She greeted me with that big beautiful smile she had and then made me feel like a million bucks when she hugged me saying, "Agosto Mio, Agosto Mio." She never expressed herself to me like that in Old Boston when I was there, but I think I knew why she didn't behave that way at the time. Deep within that hard, cold and stern exterior that Nonna so splendidly exhibited was a heart of gold filled with love for the family that few people noticed, a love that was uncompromised and not corrupted by the hard realities of life she faced every day.

Ti Amo, Nonna. Ti Amo Sempre.

978-0-595-45030-5
0-595-45030-X